cauterized

cauterized

laura apol

Michigan State University Press ▪ *East Lansing*

Michigan State University Press
East Lansing, Michigan 48823-5245

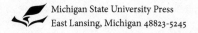

LIBRARY OF CONGRESS CATALOGING-IN-PUBLICATION DATA
Names: Apol, Laura, 1962– author.
Title: Cauterized / Laura Apol.
Description: First edition. | East Lansing : Michigan State University Press, 2024.
Identifiers: LCCN 2023031588 | ISBN 9781611864854 (paperback) |
ISBN 9781609177553 (PDF) | ISBN 9781628955187 (ePub)
Subjects: LCSH: Women—Poetry. | Grief—Poetry. |
Mothers and daughters—Poetry. | LCGFT: Poetry.
Classification: LCC PS3601.P64 C38 2024 | DDC 811/.6—dc23/eng/20230711
LC record available at https://lccn.loc.gov/2023031588

Cover design by Erin Kirk
Cover art credit: Adobe Stock / Muzi pear studio

Visit Michigan State University Press at *www.msupress.org*

For Ron
(1960–2022)

Cauterize:

To burn or freeze the skin or flesh around a wound, typically to stop heavy bleeding or to prevent the wound from becoming infected.

Contents

cauterized

i

Vanishing Point

If I go back to the place it begins: a black-and-white
tom, trains rattling my crib. When I stand,
I can see to where the tracks disappear. One day
the cat is gone; *gone*, they say, but somehow I know
the sad bundle I see between the rails
is what I have lost. And I bury
the memory for fifty years until my own dog
goes missing. She is the last thing
among last things, and I know she has been taken
by the trains. For seven miles I walk the tracks, fingering
the leather leash in my bag. The rails are higher
than I imagined, the ties spaced wrong. I expected grass
through flat fields, not these sharp stones,
not steep embankments; not trains bearing down:
hot metal, the ground shuddering, the whistle's
weight. Pain is a bargain with the gods—as if I can resurrect;
as if that old dog could run the twenty miles, thirty, forty,
ninety miles to home, could follow the tracks, the smell
of the trains, a whistle echoing what she heard in her sleep
for so many years. As if that old dog
could follow her love to me. I call her name
across pastures and woods, back yards and empty lots,
picture her running to my voice,
running toward me down the tracks. I can see
to the horizon, to the place where the rails come together,
almost out of sight.

Stigmata

I can't stop finding things
to save:
the orange kitten I feed with a dropper,
a painted turtle on the lane, the brown-needled
saplings in a row along the drive.
Each morning I carry buckets of water,
certain I can bring back green. There were winters
I knocked early snow from the lower limbs
of a fifty-foot fir, thinking I mattered.
Last summer it was monarchs, dozens of them—
caterpillars to chrysalides to wings.
There is no end to the ways

pets need me, plants need me,

men need me   to make things right
after a bad health report, a difficult colleague,
a lying girlfriend, breast cancer in a true love.
Didn't see the headlights or the brake lights
or the semi bearing down; didn't read the currents
in the river. Didn't know the headache was
the heart racing was the late nights or the slurred
speech. And how.

Each week, when my sad father calls, I am the good
girl I have been since childhood, full-on audience
since my mother died. I could have fixed him
if he'd let me. Now I am happy just to make him
happy, to be the rapt mirror for

his need   because

I know I can save the listless kitten,
the pencil-thin pines, all those lonely
men—*tell me your story,*   can hold out
        my scarred palms
to the one who misses me, though we haven't
met; the one who's never felt so fully
understood; the one who says
I remind him of his dead mother dead
wife favorite aunt first love. So when he phones,
I answer
and listen, sure this time I can fill

that unfillable hole in my father's heart.

Opening the Field

The frost heaves rocks to the surface each spring
and all through my childhood we pick them,
dropping them into the tractor bucket
of the old John Deere. Or the tilling disturbs them;
through loosened soil, they rise
and we carry them to the edge of the field. Together,
they form a rock garden. Together, they form a wall.
It is no secret that my father and I do not see eye to eye.
We have learned to route around our difference
—water seeking least resistance—though it is harder
each year. Which of us stands on the right side
of history? Now he is going door to door for the census:
Responder al censo es importante. Dale forma a tu futuro.
His Spanish is faultless; they will trust him, he says.
I say they are right to be suspicious.
Many do not have papers, are here for the farms:
seasonal planting, weeding, picking; or for the animals:
birthing, feeding, slaughtering, packing.
Some send money to relatives back home. Some
have children. They have reason not to trust.
Can you be certain, I ask my father, that no one
will come for them? He is certain. He believes.
I believe, too—that everything rises,
however buried. No matter how often we lift, carry,
remove—another frost, another tilling, another heave.
Year after year, we break ourselves on it.

Blood

—PHNOM PENH, 2016

So much need and we were there—my son and I—
to see the ruins. There were babies, women,
carts carrying animals alive and dead. Bottles of petrol.
Cigarettes. And, of course, the temples: such stone
grandeur in decay, such jostling for a photo, a moment,
a sunrise, a view. And what, after all, could we give
back? We ate street food, tipped workers and drivers
more than the guidebooks said we should. Even so,
a dollar was just a dollar. Until he read about a shortage
of blood—road crashes, maternal hemorrhages,
genetic disorders in children. Those who gave
gave for people they knew
                    but what of the rest and so

my son—my grown son who couldn't
give blood at home because he was my gay son—
led me to a clinic with a sign: *Give Blood Give
Love*. Side-by-side chairs; my beautiful boy, needle
in his arm, squeezing squeezing the sponge ball. O-
negative. He's the universal donor. After: T-shirts,
cookies, juice; they told us if we sometime needed blood
we now had bags reserved, our blood always
still our own. Outside in the heat, the stench of streets
we were on edge and newly wary: crosswalks,
traffic, buses wary; motos, taxis, tuk-tuks wary
—fearful of a need
                    to take back what had just been given.

Navigation

Before setting sail, he phones,
says *Mom, we have no ocean*
in us, means

the generations he has known
have lived landlocked, far
from water

forgetting
the months he sailed my saline,
navel-tethered;

forgetting
we are from a line of seafarers,
Dutch traders, the Zuider Zee, Noordzee,
Nederlands-Indië—

our cargo
a history
of mothers ceding sons to the sea;

forgetting
that at five he loved dolphins,
the ancients' *fish with a womb,*

studied their habits—breaches
and depths, slaps,
clicks, and whistles—

told me they transport drowning sailors
to the surface; birth their young

swimming; bond
fiercely and long.

Is Touch

Tonight I am thinking of those things
I didn't know I should love: cicadas, dragonflies,
and the birr of owls on nights I can't sleep;
the turtle on the road—a red-eared slider—
that set the dog barking; a pair of milk snakes twined
in the rock garden; wildflowers that are weeds and weeds
that are wildflowers, the forever-burrowing of moles,
and the chipmunk the mama cat brought to her young
where their instinct set upon it, tiny teeth and claws,
left only the tail. I am thinking of someone from long ago
who still knows me in my dreams. I should never have said
goodbye. What I miss most is touch, so if you come for a visit,
I will meet you on the lane. It's been so long, and at last
I have learned to hold out my hands, to say *yes*
to what I love.

Spectral

My daughter in third grade taught me
about rods and cones, short waves, long waves—
color is just light, reflected, she said; *a sensation*
in your eyes. Back then, I argued
    color is color:
the fire engine's red; the sky's blue; sunflower
yellow butter yellow lemon mustard canary
yellow.   Only now, some twenty years on,
do I read what she tried to explain:
tetrachromacy, non-spectral color
and the hues between. Ultraviolet range—

bird vision.   So when light reflects
on the hummingbird's throat, belly,
wing, I see only what I am made for—
a bull tethered to red, cave cricket, star-nosed
mole, dog napping in a shades-of-gray
world.   The limits of sight.
I try to conjure that fourth primary,
    sensation plus:
the tingle of fern, brush of apricot, chafe
of magpie. Lilac's sigh. And my daughter,
that long scorch of meteor—burning,
then gone.

Sowing with Salt

Ocean brine. Seawater.
Salt of the earth.

What is the cost for a mother looking back?

—Salt flats. Salt fields.—

I carry with me
her handwritten notes and piercings,

Hey-Mama-Bear voicemails
I will never delete

—salt mines, salt lick, salting the soil.—

For a time, I wished only to become her:
shampoo and clothes
my skin, my hair the scent of her,

my self her self

—sowing—

a daughter's name
brimstone on my tongue.
All of me the wound.
All of me, salt.

ii

Ode to the Heron

If we . . . for once could do nothing,
perhaps a huge silence
might interrupt this sadness
of never understanding ourselves

—PABLO NERUDA, "KEEPING QUIET"

Someone should tell the trees
we are sheltered in place. Someone
should tell the heron, and the light
on the heron.

Someone should tell the wild hyacinths,
the beaded grace of the willow: *this is the year*
for unfettered beauty. Do not hold back.

Consider the lilies. Consider the robin,
the redbud and forsythia. Consider
the possum, the vole, the feral cat
poised at the verge.

Praise the immovable river rocks,
bones of the fallen fir. Bless the iridescent green
beetle. Step gently.

And study the heron—   she flies
where she will   head forward, full-on

wings herself in reverse
to slow,   stop
then settle
                serene and unblinking
in the fast-moving current.

desire

the magnolia, with her honey voice,
takes in the waning moon, the last blush
of winter. she is praying
to the early gods of april, pressing her stippled
branches toward the sky, sighing her love
sigh. what she wants is to be heard—oh crocus, oh
snowdrops,
                                oh daffodils open to morning.
inside her, songbirds and stones.

Missed

The light arcs across the lawn
like the curved ribs of a violin,
slides into clefs and notes
until, in memory, my daughter
stands,   still-life,
bow in hand. No instrument.
And where is my violin? she asks.

I gave it away, I reply.
I didn't think you were coming back.

A cardinal breaks the silence then,
a farm dog down the road, barking,
and distant gunshots—
rural   recreation
on a Sunday afternoon.

What do I know
about guns?   Circle-targets
pinned to a bale, a beer can
balanced on a post.   My girl
with a Smith and Wesson
in a duplex by the Bay.

Too bad, she says.
I was thinking I should practice.

After Her Daughter Died

she bought shoes—not her usual, flat
and black, but spangled stilettos,
studded boots, strappy sandals.
She wore her new shoes
with everything—rotated by day
not by outfit, and never by event.

She teetered through the grocery store
—aisle after aisle—
blisters forming, breaking, weeping;
said aloud, *So, are you happy now?*
See what you made me do?

Why, Then, Do I Feel Such Loss?

There were years when blood was all I wanted, so afraid I would be found out. Watched for, longed for, prayed for blood—*please god* my monthly rosary.   And years I didn't want to bleed, held each month a different hope: named and rocked it, cradled changes that would change my life. Until the hoping washed away; another month, another.   Post-partum bleeding, red then pink then clear, following my firstborn—emptied womb, placental wound. Infant son in arms, I didn't know how the mother-center of me wept.   Bright blood accompanied my daughter, car too slow, elevator ride too long, gown tying in a place I couldn't reach, doubled as I was, pain pushed in splotches on the tile. *The baby's dying*—sure she had let go, certain I had failed her in a scarlet rush.   And years I bled so hard I couldn't sleep, couldn't run a mile, sit through dinner, teach a class. *Someone's hurt here; someone's hurt*—I rinsed clothes, washed sheets, made apologies for mattresses, the car's seat, office chairs.

Now, the blood is ended. *Endometrial ablation*, bleeding burned. Gone, the flow that kept the rhythm of my months, the choices of my years. Only scars within, as brined as leather, stripped and smooth and, mercifully, unworried.

Never the River

—ON THE GRAND RIVER; JUNE 21, 2020

Solstice, and over Asia there's an annular
eclipse, a bright ring of fire, corona haloing
the empty circle of sun. Here, the first day of summer
is a corona of sameness, more social distance,
unseasonably warm. A bad day for sapling pines;
a good day for crows. In a murder
they circle an imperial hawk, chase it from their trees,
black caws darkening the sky. The longest day,
and a boat motors my river after sunset. Lights,
voices across the water. *What can they catch after dark?*
And what, after all, is mine? Not the steelhead or walleye
or smallmouth bass. Not the tree frog or the evening bats
over the reeds. Not the crows fanning the last embers
of day. And never the river. The fishing men don't know
I am listening—last color drained from the sky now;
muddy smell of water and air. From here on, our days
will be shorter. From here on, less light. *Move on,*
I want to tell them. *Move on.* The sun has gone down
and the river is pushing—always pushing—
downstream.

Seated Photo of My Mother at Eighteen

I want to lean into the woman in the white Adirondack
as boldly as she leans back, dark lipstick and pin curls,
sleeveless pale blouse, slim arms wrapping her own waist—
and her smile. That irrepressible smile.
She is Fourth of July fireworks, sunflower turned toward
the sun, and I am somewhere deep within her,
swaddled in a future so far off she can barely dream it.
She is so goddamned happy, and so young. How long
before her beautiful cells will begin undoing themselves,
myelin dissevering, nerves ruined and raw?
When is the outset, the unseen scarring before the scars?
There will be decades between this Adirondack
and the electric-powered chair—years when she'll roll down
her socks, roll up her skirt, make the world hers,
until one day she no longer feels pain and the sole clue to *too hot*
or *too close* or *too much* is the smell of her own flesh, scorched.
Those glorious arms. I want to lean into this stranger
in the white Adirondack, head-thrown-back laughing.
So goddamned happy.   So young.

The First Night We Leave My Mother at Crowne Pointe

By the time I arrive from states away, my father
has hung a finch feeder outside her window
and a new seaglass mobile over her bed, arranged
her shoes, set out family photos.

Crowne Pointe, Sunshine Circle, Room 602.

Daytime is not so hard;   she has her own TV
with her own remote, door open
and every few hours a volunteer
brings cookies and juice. No, it's the night—

Forty-three years, for better or worse.
I guess this means he doesn't want to be married
anymore.

She says it surly, hurt   to hurt.

I undress her then, slide her worn nylon gown
over her head, help her into the narrow bed
by the wall, fix the covers just-so, pillow just-so,
radio just-so; kiss her forehead, leave
the bathroom door opened a crack for light,

drive with my father back to their house.
We feed her cats, stay up late saying nothing.

I wish then he was still a smoker
or that there was a bottle of Jack hidden
in a high cabinet—something to ease
the over-bright hallways, the interminable
walk to the car;   to erase
Sunshine Circle with its no cats and no double
bed and no comforter-that-matches-the-curtains,
its no Mother's Day lilac in the yard.

My father goes to their room alone. I light
a candle, watch house-moths
sputter in the melted wax.

Hershey's, 1972

The metal opener pierced two clean triangles in the tin
with a sharp snick and sigh, and we poured the Hershey's

syrup into milk: Carnation-instant-powdered, clumpy
and mixed with a wooden spoon. We drizzled

Hershey's over Betty Crocker cakes, toaster waffles
and snap-crackle-pop cereal. My father made supper

on nights my mother went to class, and oatmeal
or canned peas or popcorn counted as a meal

as long as there was dessert—Hershey's over ice cream,
blended in a mug with a wire whisk.

His was a legendary sweet tooth. He never told us
of his growing up, his fend-for-himself childhood

while his widowed mother worked,
or the lard-and-sugar sandwiches he carried to school.

He never told us that somewhere one could buy
already-chocolate cereal, ice cream ribboned with fudge,

or frothy chocolate milk, liquid-smooth.
And when the can with the sticky triangles ran empty,

my father added water, swirled and shook. Somehow,
he always could make more.

Bridges

Summers, my father built bridges. He came home
weekends, cement dust graying his hair, stories of his hard-
drinking foreman, Joe Elliot, the two of them shoveling
concrete into forms. Christensen Brothers Construction:
torn shirts and cigarettes, the crew sleeping off a bender.
The guys called my father "Prof"—couldn't believe
he didn't drink or swear, wouldn't join them

for a beer. My mother cared only that it brought in extra
cash to pay the mortgage; my brother was too young to care
at all. But I listened, awed and invisible. The unshaved,
unwashed crew loomed large, but with each telling,
my father grew larger—how he'd outpaced men a decade
younger, then two, modelling hard work and steel-toed
holiness: clean living, iced tea, cold cuts on Wonder

bread. All over Iowa, he knew the bridges that were his,
and he'd drive us out of our way to see them. Not railroad
trusses or suspension bridges; just the kind that take a soul
across a stream, a culvert, a dry creek bed. Across
a county line. I've read how bridges breathe
with the weather—expansion joints, gaps we'd panic over
if we knew it, picturing splits so wide they'd certainly

give way. His bridges were my transport out:
men and language, whiskey dreams. But I traverse
those spans on visits, follow back roads home.
Today, we take a drive. My father, now the passenger,
still fills the car with words. *Have I told you about*
the summers I worked road construction? he begins. And I say,
Tell me about them again, Dad. Tell me about your bridges.

But Winter

The tree drops apples—soft thuds through the night—
and each morning, in the late-August dappling

the deer are gathered, eating up sweet-bruised
autumn. This morning, too. But nearer the house,

a doe and a yearling nuzzle, the doe slow-licking
the fawn—face, ears, neck. From the window,

I am not amazed at the doe; what catches my breath
is the fawn, so still, her raised head, turning

toward, leaning in. A primal *yes*. We live
on a moving edge, under stars that have long ago

gone out. I still turn toward a blond flash
in a crowd; the dog rouses expectantly

at a dead girl's name. This season: for a moment,
it holds promise. A doe. A fawn. But winter—

always winter on the way.

December Crossing

I cannot capture in a photo
the doe crossing the river at dusk—
one step,
    another,
            another,

dark water touching her underside;
slender legs,

        delicate hoofs
            finding the rocks
            and mud below.

No, I cannot capture the doe,

so instead I want to be
    on the far side of the river
            when she reaches it—

to stroke her soaked fur, the silk
of her ears, her exquisite
neck.   I want

to nuzzle her forehead, my face
to her face,

to know what she knows

    about river
    about winter
            and sunset—

what to take over, crossing;
what to leave behind.

iii

Graft

My mother was fifty-six when she got her new eyes—
corneal transplants. Waiting for a donor her age,
she had us scour the paper each morning for area deaths,
guilty with hope.

Six then, Hanna worried that her grandmother,
new-eyed, would no longer know us,
would search instead for some other family—
love, inscribed in the cells.

When the time came, she ticked the donor line
on her first driver's license. Talked of it, even.

A decade later, in the wild questionings
of grief, I never asked whether anyone had remembered
to *harvest*. Hanna's heart went with her, ruined beyond
repair, but what of the rest? Liver, kidneys, lungs—

do the organs I once harbored now live
in another? I have a box of her: bone, ashes, dust.
Yet somewhere, her eyes—

Mani-Pedi

I bought it for her in middle school: a small suitcase,
lavender, with sparkles; a mirror inside the lid.
Her portable salon. She did my mother's nails:
Want a manicure, Grandma?—soaked and filed
and filled and colored. Base coat, top coat,

bent forward, blond hair falling over her face,
intent on each stroke and today I open
the suitcase. Three years, five months. I count
on my fingers. She wanted to polish my nails and I
wouldn't let her, didn't want it, no need,

and there's remover here, still, and things new
to me: brushes and files, emery boards of all shapes
and textures, toe separators, cuticle softener,
pumice, InstaDri, strengthener, hardening glaze.
My mother loved pastel pink, shell pink, coral

and peach. Here is Cloud 9, Charming, Pearl, Satin
Slip. Hanna went for blacks, reds, blues, purples
and greens. I line up the bottles: Crème Noir, Hot
Wasabi, Shock Value, Raspberry Fizz, Wild Card,
Shiver, Frenzy . . . The glitter and decals and bling.

Want a mani-pedi, Mom? I choose Crimson Fury.
Begin with my toes.

And I Can't Delete Her Voicemail Messages, Even after All These Years

Those last words, curled like
a fist, like an infant's ear, like

the head of a fern
—such a long-ago fern.

Paleolithic.
Her voice, too: insect in amber,

window onto the past. Frozen
in resin: some kind of beauty.

Some kind of death.

Why I Hate Living Alone

It is that kind of day, midsummer hot
and humid. Mornings, I open the house
to the damp of river,
pick sweet peas, feed kittens,
water the black-eyed Susans
and the door—bang bang
bang—is tiresome so I prop it open.
It is that kind of day, and a small bird,
brown and innocuous,
a house finch perhaps, female, flies
through the open door onto the porch.
Window glass all around and she
is frantic confused—the sky, the trees
so brilliantly *right there*, her own
wings beating wildly against into toward
into against toward what she knows,
the world of oak, beech, poplar—
hurtling from ledge to table to window to
desk to window to ledge. The room
is alive with her terror, and I am
frozen by her frenzy until I hear, over
the panic, not this bird but another,
perched on the rail of the deck, reddish
head thrown back, brimming
with warble, a clarion summons
—repeated, repeated, repeated, repeated—
as if he could sing her back into the sky.

Un Sospiro

Liszt's étude is a sigh, hand over hand crossing—the melody
like water, like breath. My son practiced at the spinet in the living
room, hardwood floors, and late at night the arpeggios were a river
through my dreams. The scales that fall, and fall, two hands in
parallel, descending. The first purchase I made for our new house,
that spinet. The first purchase he made for his own house, a baby
grand. *Guess what I bought, Mom.* How Liszt accompanied those years,
Beethoven, Chopin, Schumann filling the silence. Rachmaninov.
I couldn't hear what he heard—the melodic line moving through
cascades of notes, but somehow he found it, helped me learn. He was
so young the first time: car radio, long drive; he pointed out themes
that repeated, how they came around, overlapped, came around
again. One summer, I dropped him at camp, sat beside him
in a stone hut in the woods while he practiced on a concert grand.
Winters, he begged a key to a nearby church, cut the fingertips
out of gloves, played to an empty sanctuary, a space heater at his side.
Always his best audience, his sister and I sat through contests and
recitals, held our breath when he got to the section that tripped him
up, exhaled as his fingers found the notes. Later, home from college
for the holidays, he filled the house again, melodies far into the night.
The last time I had the spinet tuned, it had been years. The technician
pulled the fallboard, moved the music shelf. Showed me where mice
had unraveled a mitten, rewoven it into a nest.

Quarantine Fatigue

I can't tell what the puppy is carrying as she returns to the house, but I do note how proudly she is prancing along the walk, how gently she pads along on her enormous puppy feet. She is growing into such a good dog, a creature of sticks and stones deposited on the deck. I am not surprised when something falls from her open mouth. It is small and round; no clatter of black walnut or green apple, just a soft dropping. By the time I reach her, the treasure is hidden once more; even a treat in exchange is of little interest. Until I find something she finds worth swapping for, and she leaves it: a mole—pink feet, pink nose—tiny, wet, and dead. The mama cat is teaching her kittens to hunt, so this is someone else's prize—kitten, cat. There was a time when I would have stopped, *did* stop the cat from killing—intervened. I am tired of loss. More tired of preventing loss, imagining I can keep from happening what is bound to be. Geese fly overhead; the puppy is distracted by wings. I put her in the house, return the dead mole to the grass, where whatever will be, will be.

Sentience

When the young men sang to the elephants,
I thought it was about love. With you,
the word *love* is unspoken; we find other ways
to name what we do. This morning
the Nobel Prize was awarded
for experiments in touch, the heat of it,
which reminds me of the non-touch years
I have just come through.
Now I'm a slow burn, waking—red vines
twining the spruce. Each day
the dawn is later, the dark longer,
and we are edging closer
to far away. *I will miss you*, I imagine
saying, but I don't—say it, I mean,
I hold my tongue. I thought
it would be the changing seasons
that undid us—summer to fall; instead,
it is our speaking of elephants.
Do you really believe they don't feel?
When the young men kneel on those great backs
and sing, do you think it is only about sound?

Locks

A ship is not a kiss. Not a kiss—
just a late tanker passing, 3 a.m., moon on dark
water. But the dockside men fishing through the night
believe in love. And the lone woman watching the ship,
watching the fishing men, the rippled moonlit path—
she, too, believes. A train follows tracks laid years ago,
over rock, over field.   *Again, again, again*—
the sound of wheels grinding steel. What can she write
that has not already been written? The woman
conjures happier endings: strangers who meet on a pier;
poached eggs and toast in a diner that is never closed.
And love—   what is love
but a low-thrumming freighter, laden with cargo
as the locks lift,   and lift,   and lift
to release.

Twins

When I ask my father the story of my birth, he tells me about the car he was driving, and while it's not the story I'd hoped for, I listen. It's a start. Because what I want to know is the story not of me but of my mother, and of the twin, stillborn, and what it might have been like to have a sister, mirror-image, the other half of every conversation I never had. The car was a '58 Plymouth, light green, with bench seats and a radio that only sometimes worked. He'd listened to ball games driving back and forth to school, and the Yanks were playing the Giants in the Series that year. My mother was already at the hospital—a first, but unexpected, baby born dead—when he got the call; only then did he know there had been, would never be, twins.

But what he thought of as he drove to her was baseball, the new team he'd picked up on: the Twins. And no one spoke of my sister again. Until a decade later, when we moved to the Twin Cities and I overheard someone say to my mother, "but Gladys, *you* had twins" and she said, "yes," and I pestered her until she told. In those years, he took my younger brother and me out to see the games—Metropolitan Stadium, Hammerin' Harmon and Rod Carew—sat us in the cheap seats, insisted we wear our plastic mitts in case a fly ball was hit to deep center field. No ball ever was, but each summer I sat with my hand gloved, mitt ready. Waiting. *When you were born, people offered their condolences*, my father concludes. And he laughs.

Third Avenue

In that house it was always God: the painted brown cabinets, cornucopia wallpaper, gold and tan geometry of rugs. In that house: a Bible, worn covers, prayer, and a piano with a hymnal, the radio playing God. In that house it was always God and I dusted the mopboards each Saturday in a living room no one used. No one. God was that house, trees dying of Dutch elm disease; peonies and hollyhocks and my father's raised voice and my mother's raised hands, and all the ways I was required to confess repent forgive. A nest of wasps under the second-story eave; a leak in the cistern; mildew in the cellar where shelves were heavy with glass jars of green beans, applesauce, tomatoes, and pears. The Holy Ghost lived in the attic with the slanted roof, wandered in and out of my closets on sultry summer nights. *What is your only comfort in life and death?*—a catechism I recited at the kitchen table, but I was sleepless with the worry I was going to hell. That wood-burning stove; my father split logs, my mother fed the flame, together they cleaned soot from the chimney each fall. Bicycles and bloody knees; the pea gravel driveway, wire clothesline, spirea hedge. Summers, I watched storms move in, tossing the trees. Thought *Jesus is coming again.*

Honor

—FOR GRACE, 6/5/1914 – 12/26/1935

Her brothers did it to save her good name
because of the not-bleeding, no monthly;
did it at home, and after, brought my grandmother,
who cradled her
in what had been their shared bed—her younger
sister in a hemorrhage that left the mattress
soaked—
    all that blood   because no doctor, because
    what would the neighbors, because   *family*;
held her until her bleeding, her breathing
stopped.

From then on, my grandmother was lost.
No Grace who'd slept beside her, arm flung
wide in sleep, fighting over
    covers.   No whispered   secrets
or sister-tantrums or borrowed hairbrush or
hand-me-down shoes. No sit-beside
at Sunday dinner or walk to town.
    No someday
    come for coffee, hold the baby, recipes traded,
    peaches canned.

And the brothers—did they put on
coveralls and boots, milk the cows, butcher
chickens, bring in wood for their mother's
cookstove   *as if nothing*—
and later say their prayers before bed,
        each inventing a story
that would harden into   silence
like a husk, a shell, a pebble-hard seed, until at last
they could swallow it   or they could spit.

iv

Inferno

Ladybird, Ladybird, fly away home.
Your house is on fire, your children all gone.
—CHILDREN'S NURSERY RHYME

In the morning mirror,
the house around me is ablaze.
It's only the neighbor's maple at the window,
on fire with autumn and the early sun,
but it shocks me to know how close I am
to such flame.

Just in from across the world, jetlagged,
I look older than I thought.
Friction burn. While I was away,
the almost-grown children
found the serrated edges of their world:
it was their father, hungry ghost—

daughter, too much a woman;
son, too much a man who understood
what needed to be done, stepped between.
He used to do that for me
when he was young and I could not
keep him from it.

Back then
I thought I could save them,
though it seems I only banked the fire,
put off the day the old man
would turn us all, like kindling, to ash.
Those flames in the mirror—

Oh Ladybird,
Ladybird.

Hurricane Hanna

I keep finding smaller and smaller caterpillars
—monarch larvae the size of a pencil lead—
and this morning I started collecting
the eggs. So many in the garden; so few
pull through.
            life-threatening   *high risk*
It's sunny today so I put them on the porch
where I have cookie sheets, netting,
mesh cages and a supply of fresh milkweed
that they daily strip down
to the stems.
            force of nature   *critical*
I'd like to imagine this as an act of love.
Mostly, I'd like to imagine I can avoid
the news.
            landfall
            storm surge   *torrential rain*
                    natural disaster
It's good-joke funny if a hurricane
shares a name with your daughter when she's alive.
But she is not, and it sends me to the milkweed
to drown out the words.
            deluge   *downpour*
                                    unleashing
She loved Padre Island, where her father
took her—   took her
summers, where this hurricane is making
landfall right now.
            eye of the storm
            catastrophically dangerous
A perilous world. So many predators;
such slight defense.

a friend asks if i believe in heaven

while i am not watching,
the monarch splits her chrysalis skin, emerges,

wings pulsing for flight. so ready, so flutteringly
ready. i hold out to her

the intimacy of lavender and she steadies,
accepts. to the breeze then—

a prayer as she takes the sky, lifts into blue as if
it is hers. the far scent of blossom. as if.

Regret

It was my clavicle you loved best, blue-tinged
shadow at the base of my throat, a place you said
tasted of lemons and rain. That day in the woodshed,
rusted trowel in hand, I told you about the bloodied lip
and you told me about your new life. I wasn't ready yet
to go. But way leads on to way: a gravel drive
and a red wheelbarrow to a path over the stream,
the empty field stretching beyond. I want you
to know: our orioles return each May; as always,
I slice oranges, put out sugar water. They leave each June—
one morning I realize they are gone. After so many years
I am still surprised.

At the Edge of Sixty, Autumn

and I'm thinking of Demeter, Persephone,
and those pomegranates at the health food store,
how I wish they'd ripen sooner.
Because I want to give one to Michael,
a man I've just met whose name collides
with history. My history. I could call him Mike,
but my brother's name is Mike. He's a lawyer. Or Mick,
but I know a Mick from childhood. Mick's a doctor.
When we were in kindergarten, Mick stuck his head
through the slats of a wooden chair. The janitor saved him
with a hand saw. Mick never lived it down—
but truthfully, what *do* you live down? Or live up to?
Expectations. My parents never wanted me
to be anything but saved. Is that expectation
too high or too low? I might still be saved
in the eleventh hour, that sweet spot just before
the grave. *Pomegranates,* I want to tell Michael,
signify death but also fertility. So where is the sweet spot
in this? A daughter's distance, mother's mourning,
earth-fallow days. Or passion, perhaps—insatiable
hunger, those jeweled ruby seeds an aphrodisiac
rousing the tongue.

January, Pandemic

                    and the gibbous moon
enters the room through bare trees,
branch-shadows crossing the unslept
side of the bed.   I name, rename
the light: *Luna* to *Lunatic*, *Loco*
to *Lobo*—which translates to *Wolf*
in the deepest hour of dark. I think
I have made the wrong mistakes: too many,
too much, too tightly   because
it's so much easier not to let go.
The insatiable *but what if.*
                    They say dreams reveal
a state of mind, so I've stopped
sharing mine,   though the one
where the car fills with water
lingers for days. Perhaps it's simply
the moon, that doppler of loss.
Last week, my father's sister
died at a distance. He told me
that after the call, he stayed
at his desk, playing solitaire online.
                    Ten months into alone,
and still I am resisting: the rising sea,
the moon-tossed bed, the yellow
lupine eye.

Offering

Today, the river is freezing over like a scar, the dark
current covered with ice, with snow, printed by talons
and delicate paws. The curves of the field fill with drifts,
cedars dark and dusted—who can I say this to? For so long
I have fashioned maps, hoping you would find me again—
a trail of white pebbles, Polaris to guide. Here, eagles *scree*
in the woods, a winter hare shrieks

and what did you save from those ravenous
afternoons? We slaked different hungers, so when the cat
brings to me a dark-eyed junco in this sub-zero
solitude, how can I say no? I still track the moon's phases,
take my coffee black. But now, my waist has thickened,
my hair, greyed—and if we meet again,
what would you make of it?

Wild geese huddle at the lip of ice; a mute swan
glides the creek-flow that does not freeze. Such stillness;
all that river beneath.

It Was the Wind

that disrupted our call, freighted and midnight-
bound. Not the coyotes across the fields.
Not the owls from the oaks. In the ravine,
bare trees creaked and moaned under the weight
of a snow-cold moon. And that
wind. It was the first I'd heard your voice
since you left, but each sentence shattered, phrases
dropped—our syllables, stilted and strange.
Fractured, you said before we gave up.
I think now of what was lost to the wind—
unsaid, or said but unheard. If what I've loved best
is your silence, was this more of it or less?
I listened, long after the line went dead,
trying to hear what I missed. I thought you said
happy. But you might have said *coffee*. Or perhaps
you said *come to me*. How would I know?

Memory and Breath

Last night I dreamed you were a fish,
                                you who never took
to water, never learned to swim.
Not salt-sculling, ocean-homed,
        but a river fish
hovering over the bed
of gravel, hugging
the rocks near the bank. I might have been
a fish too, though I am one who trusts
water, swims well, and, like a salmon,
returns—
                        all matters of memory
and breath.

Now your ailing mother
                                    has forgotten
your years of care, does not even ask
after you.   *It's fine*, you tell me
—a forgiving disease, her loosened grasp
on what has been lost.

                    But I wonder
whose *fine* is the forgetting, whose
the forgiving.   And why
you are restless in sleep, holding me
as if I could hold you
up.   We have become so skilled
at denial—the silt-record of history;

how learning to swim
                    is learning to drown.

Afterlife

The Calusa of Sanibel believed people and animals reincarnated as ever-lower forms until they disappeared altogether, like the shells turned into sand.

—SIGN AT THE CALUSA SHELL MOUND TRAIL ON SANIBEL ISLAND

True or not, I like thinking about such a return, bones
turned to shell turned to sand. Mostly, I like thinking about
this: days with no edges, the slow churn of the sea, and how
a sand dollar, perfect on the beach—whole, and wholly
a gift—washed up at our feet the morning I was headed
home. A star-flower scratched on the urchin crown, petals
etched on the underside, it was the only thing unbroken
on a beach littered with shells—shattered bones of the ocean—
and I placed it in a bag I'd brought for whatever I might save.
As we shuffled the shallows, I chose a chipped nautilus,
traced its whorls—toward or away, depending on the start—
smoothed it between my fingers and thumb. I did not ask
what I wanted to ask and you did not tell. Nearing the place
we'd parked, I turned back toward the gray-green sea,
the gray-blue sky, streaks of sunlight breaking through.
Pelicans threaded a long V over the waves, and I made a wish
before I threw the nautilus into the foam. I told you then
about coins in fountains, wishes I made. You did not ask
if those wishes came true, said simply, *so God has a price*—
statement, not question. Home the next day, I took out
what I'd packed, found the sand dollar broken to bits,
layers fragile as phyllo, strata smoother than I'd have thought.
What life, this, and what next? Each fragment I touched,
more dust, fine powder of sand. I wished it could be fixed,
edges aligned—thought how once I might have tried. Instead,
I placed the bleached shards on a porcelain plate.
The lingering grit, I brushed into the air.

V

I Take a Realtor through the House I've Lived in for Twenty-Five Years

Once again I was there and once again I was leaving
and again it seemed as though nothing had changed
even while it was all changing

—W. S. MERWIN

Windows that wouldn't open, a door
that wouldn't close;   worn-carpet room of my son,
cobalt room of my daughter,   flowered-over grave
of the backyard dog.   Sump pump, shingles,
emergency contact and every shadow
a ghost. Up these steep stairs I was young, filled
with tomorrows as I took lovers   and lit candles;   sang
with my children   and prayed   for my children,
and wept and bled each month

and it is all past.   The laundry off the line. Pears
rotting beneath the tree. Fireflies and maple leaves,
lost cat's print in concrete
like the stories I read aloud to my daughter before bed,
my son at the piano,   Rachmaninov in his sleep.
New stove, used fridge,
all the dishes I washed, lunches I packed;
push mower, extension ladder, gutters cleaned
spring and fall.   Wisteria and weeping
cherry,   heights penciled on the painted
frame of the door,   painted over.

And now?
Siding and ceiling fans, hard-wood floors and fencing;
trees   that fell

—as nothing, as everything,

changed.

Why of the Black Moon

—FOR ROXANA, LEAVING KIGALI EARLY

Because your mother is dying,
because my mother
has died,

and each new moon is a withered
womb;

because we have ceased
our prayers.

Because I have my mother's smile
and wear my mother's rings,

because you have your mother's hair,
will soon wear your mother's rings.

Tonight, the scattered lights come on—
starlight, streetlight, firelight, fireflies, fires
in these hills;

because the two-lane blacktop rises
then falls, wrapping us breathless in shrouds
of night:
        —oh, Mama—

because there is only the call, no response.

Because she is distant, the moon

and we have learned to navigate
the dark   because
she is gone.

Mothering

We met when Immaculée was still a girl. She asked me for milk.
In Rwanda, milk is a gift from the mothers.

Back then, she was so alone and could tell me her orphaned
ache, though what in god's name did I know yet about loss?

The gloss of leaves, red dirt, African warblers—
one word led to another, years into years: schooling, jobs, marriage.

I brought her pots and pans and cotton sheets, leather shoes;
books for the babies who grew beneath the stretch of her skin—

she just wanted a family,
                    blood kin to replace what machetes had taken.

I rocked infants named for her lost brothers: Avi, then Noah;
I was their first *muzungu*, white as the chalk moth, far off

as the moon. Immaculée wrote today to tell me
the new baby, Joseph, had come early, infection, would not

last the night. *I need your comfort*, she wrote; *I wish to tell you*
my story. I lie and say I am praying.

But where is that god who watches the sparrow? Such hunger;
so little bread.

In Time

After her death, my mother came back
as an eagle. I saw her often.
You saw her too. Once, home
from college, childhood ornaments
arranged on the family tree,
you stood at the window, gazing out
at the river when *—Look—*
a dark shape flew close, turned
into the wind. When the sky went slate-
empty again, you said, *That's how*
I'll always see Grandma. And you asked,
How do you think we'll see Grandpa?
And later,

I will see you *in everything.*

I knew then that when someday
I came to you, you would know me
and it made me glad—the ordinals
of loss and my sure return, forever,
to you. I never wondered how you
might return to me. *My daughter,*
now sea turtle, hummingbird,
monarch; now yellow-eyed heron
at the river's edge, rare, and relentlessly
still. *Look—* what memory, water.
What memory, sky.

Elegy

as the hart
as the salmon
as the luna moth

yearns

as the ibis
as the ivy
as the sea turtle

yearns

as the mother-milk breast
as the lone twin

yearns

as the gate swung open
and the gate grown shut

as rain without thunder
storm without rain

and rain
and the rainbow

and the parched field

yearns

so my heart

oh daughter
so daughter, my heart—

Gift

The meaning of life is that it stops

—FRANZ KAFKA

Steeped in grief,
    I longed for even a glimpse
                        of brightness—
hibiscus chords, hovering;
                trumpet vines;
emerald plumes and a ruby
thrum.

    I put out sugar water.

Jazz, the calico,
    reading my desire
                in the morning
laid at the door
        a perfect blossom: iridescent
    wings,
a clotted crimson throat.

Prayer in the Time of COVID

I invite a friend to dinner: roasted cauliflower,
chickpeas and kale. We eat outdoors, six feet
apart. She is too thin; tomorrow
she will start radiation. They will tattoo
markers across her breasts—
a constellation permanent as the Pleiades.
She tells me how, one Thanksgiving, her son
made a salad of kale he massaged in the kitchen,
kneaded to tenderness. The power of touch,
she says. I say I have not been touched
since March—not a brush of skin, bumped
elbow, side-by-side thigh. All week
there has been a giant silk moth
laying eggs on the screen door in back,
so near I could have stroked her wings. I think
of the hands that create a radiologist's map,
that break down the veined leaves of the greens
or worship the unblinking eyes imprinted
on wings. *God of the haloed virus that brings us*
to this, read our upturned palms—each fingerprint
so singular; each so holy and so strange.

still, life

blue, says bowl—the color
of sleep. take your hand, says bowl;
together we will womb to ripeness
peaches, their smooth skin,
the soft fuzz of touch. you hold me; i hold them
here in the sweet sheen of evening.
make a cradle, says bowl. sing lullaby
and cream.

vi

Cradlesong

And then came piecing myself back together
—gardens I tended that did not
say no; tides that brought gifts.
There are words for offspring: fledgling,
cygnet, kitten, cub. What made me think
I could name her—she, fully formed:
toenails, elbows, lashes and lungs, already
a hole in her heart. She could finish my stories
—tell it in my ear, Mommy—
could predict what followed, each next line.
You made it, she said, never affirmation,
only accusation: the star, the shelf,
the melody, falling. She wanted to be
like me, be not me, always a note
I could not rise above, can never refuse:
sing, Mommy; sing.

If Birds, April

The field is filled with birdsong. Bird-
song, wildflowers, and bones.
Under the cedar, black hoofs and fur
tell of a long winter. Near the hawthorn,
a jumble of tail feathers
and wings. I am used to finding carcasses
in spring; today, the husk of a foil balloon
is snagged along the ravine—
a sapphire surprise.
                                        Always, this is for me
a season of loss—memory
in the ache of green, the robin's return.
What kind of message, then,
this sudden mylar blue? Such wild skin,
gossamer in the rain. Across the path,
a young kit shelters beside the barn.
But you're just a baby, I say aloud to her. *Just
a baby.*
                                        Golden repair—*kinsugo*—
the art of piecing together what has been
broken. More beautiful mended
than before the breaking, I will never be.
Under the eaves, a phoebe
is patching last year's nest. Soon,
eggs. Soon, early flight.
Who can say how many lost birds
are too many?

One Magnolia

O prolong / now the sorrow if that is all there is to prolong.

—DONALD JUSTICE

Five years, and still
                        it sears
my skin,   the grief

of a heart that once grew inside me, her
breaking. Sorrow has become

my familiar.
Each spring, my body bends toward
this day, toward

that hour, in a
push,

a push
like birthing, the primal need to pray her
not to—

                        but it was never
my decision to make.

Not hers either, any more than a house
chooses

to fall in wind; any more than a finch
chooses
to fly—headlong—into a horizon
                                        of glass.

Riven

Because, of course, we can't bring back the past;
we can't bring back the dead.

—ANNE MICHAELS

This is the way water goes:

rain filters through fields, rivulets
run the ravine   to the stream,
to the river, to the Great Lake.
Follow that path; like time, it flows
only one   way. Yet

each year the salmon
reverse,

come in from the hugeness
of water,   fight the current
toward the creek, past fallen
branches, clots of twigs and rocks
and flats;

flip and flash their way over gravel,
bodies pink, then spotted
with decay. They are death, they are

life,   they are food
for scavenging eagles and foxes,
coyotes and owls, food for their own
                    spawn;
spawning, spawned—is this

a story of hope or loss? Is memory
in or *of* water? Day
after day, the fall foliage
thins,   yellow confetti shed
into the stream—

                    as if the Lake,
as if the river; as if the fox and owl;

as if the fish bones and the rainbow
skins and the empty
eyes

fed and were fed by the journey
        home
—as if the past is the future
and the ravaged salmon
        reach it—

this rock-strewn ravine, slicked
with rain;   this putrid stream,
    bright-gilded with dying
leaves.

Memoir

They are there without me
    —always there,
        or so I imagine—
basking in the half-light of memory.

There is fire in the woodstove. Ice
        on the river.

A candle at dusk. Perhaps a bit of jazz.
Would anyone care for a drink?

I have made a home for them:

my never-born
twin. My mother. My daughter.

And last night, the calico.

They are waiting for me, in a cabin
    that smells of cedar

and musk. The driveway
is long. A frozen stream
        snakes the ravine.

Each time the door opens,
            they turn, as one.

Rapture

The last day of the world will not find my father
on his knees, where he has been for so many firsts
and lasts and days between. Instead, he'll call me up.
He'll read aloud the local obituaries, repeat
a rabbi-and-priest joke he heard at morning coffee,
tell me that *Dante's Inferno* was yesterday's answer
to final Jeopardy and he got it right. He'll tell me to be sure
that the outdoor cats have enough food to get by,
that the temp-controlled condo he sent for them
is still plugged in. He'll inquire about the bat house,
the salt lick, remind me to clean the fridge and leave out
my vegetable scraps for the possums and raccoons.
On the last day of the world, my father will wander
back to stories about the girls he dated, his high school
barbershop quartet, and the grocery store he managed
the summer after my birth. Then he'll advise me
to pick all my unripe tomatoes, arrange them
on the windowsill in the sun. Just in case.
In the last moments of the last day of the world,
my father will think of the cardinals, chickadees,
hummingbirds, jays. *Are all the feeders filled*?
he'll ask. *You don't want to be someone who is unfaithful*
to the birds.

Rwanda, Twenty Years On

—FOR LOUISE, A SURVIVOR OF THE GENOCIDE
AGAINST THE TUTSI OF RWANDA

at the end of the two-decade road

is a house   tin roof   stone fence
windows still wanting for glass

and
    yes   the house
is a house and
    yes   the storm clouds
are clouds and
    yes   the cradled child

is a child   *miracle* the haze
of his hair   *miracle* the scent

of his skin   two decades ago his mother
hid in the swamps for weeks

orphan teeth   loosening
budding breasts   shriveled against
hunger's

ribs   two decades ago she
        alone
carried the future   her great-
grandmother's voice   her twin-
brothers' smiles
through bloodied days through

panic nights *there is nothing*
she says *nothing*
that can touch me now   her hand

on the curve of   the baby's
                                                her baby's

back and I take it
in   the miracle hair the rutted
road with the mud-red drive

the roof in the rainstorm
            such   bright wings

Umbra

When I sleep
the shadows of my hands
come to me

—SIV CEDERING

because I wear the rings of the dead.

because the veins
are my motherline, heat so blue.

because awake, each hand is a fish,
and in dreams,
each a bird, hollow twinning of bones.

because Liszt lives in the reach,
Vivaldi, in motion, the Trout Quintet
rippling across strings.

because I was forced to fold hands
and pray.

because splinters work their way out.

because I am quick with the needle,
tenacious with the black
unbreakable thread.

because there are scars and I forgive them.

because long ago, from his seat in the back,
my toddler son said, *Mom,*
you have beautiful hands.

Backbeat

And could you have stopped it?
I wanted to be wanted and they were
hungry. *And could you have stopped*
it? It was time. I had outgrown
it all. *And could you have*
stopped it? My mother was buried
on Leap Day; I grieve her
every four years. *And could you*
have stopped it? I said *not yet*
when I should have said *yes.*
He never asked again. *And could*
you have stopped it? Out the car
window: black dog like the night,
like the highway. Black dog. *And*
could you have stopped it? All those years
she didn't tell me didn't
tell me—why didn't she tell me?

And could you have stopped it?
An early frost. I was tired.
            Such a long, long walk.

vii

Cauterized

If I go back to the place it begins: a stillborn twin sister, trains rattling the crib. And I bury the memory for fifty years. Because I have my mother's smile and wear my mother's rings. Because my father and I do not see eye to eye. Because my parents never wanted me to be anything but saved. Call it *Friction burn*. Say *God has a price*.

How many lost birds are too many? I have learned the words for offspring: fledgling, cygnet, kitten, cub. My grown son couldn't give blood because he was my gay son; my daughter, that long scorch of meteor—burning, then gone. Where is the god who watches the sparrow? *Sing, Mommy; sing.*

The river is pushing—always pushing—downstream. Near the hawthorn, I find a jumble of tail feathers and wings. *But you're just a baby*, I say. So much easier not to let go.

I still turn toward a blond flash in a crowd, wonder if memory is *in* or *of* water. And what, after all, is mine. These days, I am tired of loss. I am more tired of preventing loss. But I believe, too—that everything rises, however buried. Because there are scars and I forgive them. Because I was forced to fold hands and pray.

Because pain is a bargain with the gods. So what life, this, and what next? Once, my father built bridges. My mother was so goddamned happy, and no one spoke of my twin sister again. Oh, daffodils, open to morning—inside, songbirds and stones.

A friend asks if I believe in heaven. Such hunger; so little bread.

Notes

PAGE 19 According to traditional Chinese medicine, there is a direct connection between the uterus and the heart.

PAGE 33 Étude No. 3 by Liszt is more commonly known as *Un Sospiro*, Italian for "a sigh." The notes rushing up and down resemble the inhalation and exhalation of breath.

PAGE 44 Hurricane Hanna made landfall on Padre Island at 5 p.m. central time on Saturday, July 25, 2020.

PAGE 48 "I have made the wrong mistakes" is a line from jazz musician Thelonious Monk.

PAGE 56 A black moon is the second new moon in a calendar month.

PAGE 71 After the W. S. Merwin poem, "Place," which contains the lines, "on the last day of the world / I would plant a tree."

PAGE 72 In Rwanda, a metal roof is a mark of security and prosperity.

Acknowledgments

If it takes a village to raise a child, it also takes a village to support the crafting of a collection of poetry. I am, as always, grateful to and for my village. During COVID, many new connections were made possible from afar; what a strange and unexpected gift in the midst of such uncertainty and loss to Zoom into readings and workshops around the world. A village, from a distance brought near. My gratitude, then, is far-reaching.

Many of these poems were started or refined at Honeymoon Bay, Lake Cowichan, British Columbia, and I'm grateful for years of friendships there: Wendy Donawa, Daniel Scott, Michelle Poirer Brown, Susan Alexander, Liz McNally, Barbara Pelman, Mary Ann Moore, Arleen Paré, Susan Braley, Linda Thompson, Anne Hopkinson, Michael Boissevane, Kate Braid, Gisela Ruebsaat, and Nancy Issenman.

Valuable feedback on the manuscript came from Shanna McNair and Scott Wolven of The Poetry Hotel. At the Bear River Writers' Conference, I was fortunate to study with Richard Tillinghast and Thomas Lynch, and found kindred spirits in Michelle De Rose and Hannah Wright Matthews, the poet-friends I'd been seeking—talented, insightful, and filled with grace and goodwill.

Special thanks for the gift of wise and incisive responses to the finished manuscript from Susan Olding and Chelsea Comeau.

Poet friends and friends who don't consider themselves poets have, as always, listened to, encouraged, and celebrated my poems; in no particular order, then, thanks to Carol Mason, Roxanne Klauka, Twila Konynenbelt, Stephanie Jordan, Stephanie Alnot, Melanie Morrison, Doug Van Epps, Beth Herbel-Eisenmann, Ruelaine Stokes, Scott Harris, Cathy Colando, and Cynthia Hockett. A village, indeed.

I am grateful for colleagues at Michigan State University, and for funding that supports my creative work. Once again, it's an honor to be working with the MSU Press, especially Caitlin Tyler-Richards, Kristine Blakeslee, and Amanda Frost. Gratitude as well to my department chair, Dorinda Carter Andrews, and to Stephanie Nawyn, director of the Center for Gender in Global Context, for so often finding ways to say "yes."

There is always a special thanks I owe to the two writer-friends from whom I've benefitted most across the years: Lorna Crozier and David Pimm. They inspire, steer, curb, and promote with steadfastness and skill. And, of course, ongoing heart-appreciation to my family: Mike and Rachelle, Brandon, Elayne and Josh, Dad and Carol.

Finally, greatest love and gratitude to my extraordinary son, Jesse; he is my most faithful cheerleader and, without question, the best thing I have done in this life. And to Hanna: I miss you fiercely, sweetie—every every day.

Thank you to the editors of the following journals, in which poems in this book, sometimes as earlier versions, first appeared:

Bear River Review: "Cradlesong," "Sentience." *Consequence Forum*: "Mothering." *Crosswinds Poetry Journal:* "Prayer in the Time of COVID," "Rwanda, Twenty Years On" (Nominated for a Pushcart Prize). *Flying South*: "Navigation." *Lansing City Pulse:* "In Time." *Michigan Quarterly Review*: "Blood." *New Guard*: "Never the River," "Offering," "It Was the Wind." *Nimrod International Journal:* "Afterlife," "But Winter," "Gift," "Honor," "Is Touch," "Memoir," "Opening the Field," "Sowing with Salt," "Spectral," "Stigmata," "Twins," "Vanishing Point." *Prime Number*: "Umbra" (Nominated for a Pushcart Prize). *Ruminate:* "Rapture." *The Shore*: "Regret." *Sixfold:* "I Take the Realtor through the House I've Lived in for Twenty-Five Years," "Seated Photo of My Mother at Eighteen." *Thimble:* "*Why* of the Black Moon." *Unbroken:* "Inferno."

"A Friend Asks if I Believe in Heaven" first appeared in *Peninsula Poets* (Poetry Society of Michigan, Fall, 2022). "Ode to the Heron" first appeared in *Power of the Pause*, edited by Heather Tosteson and Charles D. Brockett (Decatur, GA: Wising Up Press, 2022). "Riven" first appeared in *Sweetwater: Poems for the Watershed*, edited by Yvonne Blomer (Halfmoon Bay, BC: Caitlin Press, 2020).